OUR WORST

John Birtwhistle

Our Worst Suspicions

Anvil Press Poetry

Published in 1985
by Anvil Press Poetry Ltd
69 King George Street London SE10 8PX
ISBN 0 85646 131 8
Copyright © John Birtwhistle 1985

This book is published
with financial assistance from
The Arts Council of Great Britain

Photoset in Times
by Bryan Williamson
Printed in England
at the Arc & Throstle Press
Todmorden Lancs

CONTENTS

THE FLOWERING CURRANT

as though from the Chinese

1

The linnet sings
The bullrush stands again
Grey water blues again at the brim

The storm flakes out
Only the watcher is troubled still

2

A butterfly's tongue my glance
would probe every fold of a room
for her sweetness

and looks around these days
tasting of ash

3

Today received several complaints
issued few instructions
forgot about verse

Dark finds me studying
another paper alone

4

My duties take care of themselves
Decisions are made elsewhere
Many would say I ought to be content

to breathe these orange-flowers
filled with memories

5

An inner courtyard
silently walls in
her absence with a disused well

I watch from my desk
embezzling time

6

I joke somewhat stiffly
Colleagues wonder
Has he a heart in his ribs?

My heart may tremble
My back is a yardstick

7

Much of the afternoon
when I should be writing reports
I draft these lines on willow leaves

as they fall sharp
in patterns on the many paths

8

The first official
day of spring finds me
collecting fines

and the longstemmed
flowering currant in flower

9

I get noticed for the willow verse
Larger matters are not in my gift
The willow curves in its own script

Eye for detail has the say
in offices like mine

10

In this courtyard
a famous dialogue is set
and we discussed it here

Duty keeps calling me back
where I can look out for you

11

Silky sky
haze of pollen
are bringing back my thoughts

Once we were candid
and cast a single shade

12

As the peartree fails
and friends drop away
it is often the slightest things

Child's play with pebbles
The scent of rain long delayed

13

Having once passed exams
I can sit at this table
tracing name after name

and absently look up at the wall
and name what frightens me

14

My young colleague passes
his newborn son
round the table like a cheese

wishing him nothing but brains
which have done so much for us

15

Press gangs
go with my seal
along the springline villages

though I would rather protect
the poor of this world

16

I dreamed again
of the slight field
in the small of the hill

as though the edge could keep
when the knife is melted down

17

Horsemen muster on the plain
Stupid birds will soon be setting out
where I am forbidden to go

longing for here
where I used to hear you laugh

18

A brace of duck
beck and call
neither calling first

The sun a red seal
The lake a cleaned mirror

19

In another room
someone cuts fennel
an entrancing smell

Whole provinces pass
into other hands

20

The horses return
Several villages
a single plume of smoke

Even at my desk
winter sets in

21

Sickleave enables
me to linger for once
with the hundred poets

those of dispassion
those of inmost thought

22

Being reliable
I know what it means
to pass on orders

Being liable
I know what exile means

23

By a single taper
I write out an old verse
I would care to have written

dwelling on love
that bookish theme

24

Dusk
a frail bridge
I cannot put you out of mind

A skein of geese
Mist rising from the lake

25

Clear stars only recall
the alterable things
as I lie with my thoughts

Elsewhere in the house
a child cries with my voice

26

In the presence of others
you touched me on the wrist
Woken early by messages my dreams

go on and I wonder how you are
somewhere beyond in the morning

SHADOW OF THE ADVISERS

Ils disaient désirer la bonne intelligence
– Paul Eluard, 'La Victoire de Guernica' (1938)

1

The piercings would lens the wick
    of our paraffin stove
so they cast shimmering c's on the wall
        the scales of carp in a print

        on the wall that valid pastoral
    of the attacked
a distant range of hills
          a twisting trail

      in their conical hats
the peasant lines hoeing the terraced hills
    arrayed along a slogan

        A spiral staircase with broken steps

Barrels poking from shoulders
    The smell of paraffin burning in Islington
We mingled like metaphors
        figuring each
      as shadowless
      to the other

    But who can speak sufficiently of Vietnam?

      of Pacification
    and the lecture note read literally
     "the fragmentation of man"

2

The dubious idiom of our souvenirs

    flailing shadows of blades
the gunrest concealed in a slip of bamboo
    the old bringing fruit and rice
to the young tunnelling out a maze

    the thumping undertone and then
helicopter gunships with screaming blades
    the jargon for gadgets
adhesive fire perfected in Universities

        "Survivors of My Lai told yesterday
how US soldiers entered their village three times.
Twice they handed out candy to children." *

    jargon of fragging and zapping
the swampland sown with rice and mines

but once in a Cuban film
    a cow aborting in an irrigation ditch
        after an air raid
    a metal swordfish roped on a cart of wood

    after an air raid
    caught in rifle fire from an irrigation ditch
        or a cow giving birth

and so for 35 years

and tourists returning with aluminium rings
    from the shot-down plane

* Report from Saigon, *The Guardian* 20/11/69, p.3

3

and a badge
              SCIENCE FOR
              THE PEOPLE
                        with red fist
superimposed on a white hand holding
      a triangular chemical flask

      not more subtle than the fist
but recalling your
                  inflected
                        hand

the distillation of careful analysis

      no less delicate than
excellent scholars inventing napalm
            to exact specification

but this was Science for the People

      and I only ask whether
that fist was aware of that hand
                  and why
the designer could not marry them
                        and how
            the tension went unnoticed

when in the standard shot from the door
      down the sights onto wooded hills
you spotted the shot for a moment
      included the shadow

of the black dragonfly
                  from which it was taken

4

My client could hardly have come prepared
for "violence" in N. Audley Street
or why be wearing a string of beads
                    that burst across the kerb?

                    The shadow of the advisers

                    Ingenious graphic artists
evolving vivid ways to show
                    results from spyplanes

rice dumped in rivers

                    The sensitive findings
of ethnographers used to bombard
            the village structure
                    of the Mekong delta

rice poisoned rice burned

And to make another start your banner
painted without misgiving
            that a City was renamed

            hundreds fighting on office roofs
for a place on the last choppers out
            thousands fleeing along the roads
Such newsreel night by night

the clattering typescript of
"interdict" "contact" "activity" "swept"

and in the aesthetic haze of burning palms
one of the many holding
                    her child
                    dead at her breast

            her other hand clenched
                beating at each
                    step her forehead

And to make yet another start
    news of Neruda dying in arms

5

            a City renamed

"One shall give much to him who needs much;
one shall give little to him who lacks little;
one shall give nothing to him who lacks nothing;"

            our shimmering scales

"One shall take where there is abundance
        and give where there is need;
one shall compensate poor lands by rich lands." *

            The Vietcong
were correct and annoying the police correct
at the Tet offensive
                so wipe away
                those crumbs with a cloth

            and her if you can
            holding her child
the newsreel going round and round
on a loop an image overexposed
                beating
                beating her forehead

* Viet Minh principles quoted in B.B. Fall, *The Two Viet-nams*
    (London, revised 1965), p.158

the last violence that of exposure
                              O shadeless
                              Guernican lamp!
          with razing blades of light

spikes of light so solid the fire casts their shades
     bulb remorseless shadeless in its enamel cone
          Picasso's taut pupil in open slit of white

Lash those who destroy and talk of saving

Expose the latent content of these years

Pierce to the trembling shoots of becoming

6

A spiral staircase with broken steps

FROM THE FIRST

1

His schoolboy poems were full of paintings
hints of birdlife leaves or lacework
hair to oval pallid faces
eyes to follow around his room

It was they received the budding gifts
of syntax and unease
    and if one let slip
even her pronoun could be erased

leaving the lace the leaves the birds

2

He ran his fingers a latecomer through the sand
whipped into slight arcs by the wiry grasses
and came up with a cinder and a touch of rust

Spent waves   fishing sails all furled
Seapinks wandering like hedgehogs
and deeper   metal from the parents' wars

HAIL MARY

after Yannis Ritsos

Step down Our Lady of the salt fish-eyes
Of the hand smoked over by complaints of the poor
And from all the years that this has gone on

Down in rockpools love is waiting for you
The seagull hangs your sooty icon in his cave
The jealous urchin stabs up at your feet

Come lady clutching the eggs of lightning
The grandmother grasps a knife in her wrinkled pleat
The roots of the olive are on the boil

Some seablue day you will take off your scarf
Take up the daggers of your silvery sorrows
For the hail of May to strike you head-on

For sun to split as the pomegranate
On your sailcloth apron as you share out the sun
To your dozens of orphans seed by seed

Scouring the shore so it gleams like a blade
Or as the snows that glisten in spring so the crab
Comes out to sun himself and his claws cross

HAIKU

a frosty eyelash
after your swim in the sea;
and a speck of oil

DEVICE

Dear I am one distrusting his own powers
The devices and desires of my own heart
I have neglected so long
I hardly know them or where they might be kept
But what have you found
In here salted away like anchovies?

ALLEGORY
OF IMPROBABLE GLANCES

We find ourselves with an arrival
    and departure board wiped clean,

motives from a forgotten play
    posing in contrived space

Can the tint on the landing be still
    imprinting the source of light

(lilac) otherwise soluble
    in us largely as the wish

for a vineyard so startlingly
    luscious the birds ignore it

where poetry is so profuse
    we only bother with the hearts?

How these figures – pagan
    apparently – are come by is lost,

but they have the feel of joining
    and only in the pendant work,

the Frieze Of Surprisingly Light
    Casualties, can we discern

comparable lines of gaze

The technique is studied,

perhaps too fastidious for any
        calm it might intend –

except for one passage,
        the couple on the floating bridge

who lean over as they watch
        that kind of TV

which is best cause and cure
        for sleeplessness. These

form a caesura and, rewarding
        your complicity so far,

supply a satisfying fake:
        with a touch of piracy on high

literatures, they seem about
        to place in a slender bubble

that thorny paradigm
        that rhymes with disclose

and is so transient men pluck
        it out to stand for unending

BOUND ASSOCIATIONS

a tollgate cop in a circular question
half watches out
for some sweet change in the heat

for a hitch a hiker a girl to freefall here
whose rainlike frock
will billow in the slipstream of a lorry

as breathlessly she makes her break
the bar saluting
girl and lorry hauling away the heat

      +

sounds of a distant train in the night
rushing parallel
to the mountains hooting at crossing after crossing

FOR THE SURREAL DEAD

Surreal, noun, obsolete form of SURROYAL.
An upper or terminal branch of a stag's
antler, above that called 'royal'. See
George Turberville, *Arte of venerie* (1575).

1   A SANTINO OF ANDRÉ BRETON

They slip a poem largely abstract
into the pocket of his corpse
for style feeds off anything even
excuses   The husbands were away
the asset-strippers moving in
  That the phone went unanswered
shows influence of french film
    and nothing but an interview refused
    by Wish the master topiarist

In the french film an infant boy
is up to sexy doodles answering
the phone   The conical trees
voiceprint excited laughter as
adults and afternoons foregather
to uphold the institution
of Adultery in the Novel
    whilst the boy   falling asleep
     fingering   his mouth   and eyes

They slip him through the railings
I blame French Film he declares
  thrashing flowerbeds with a stick
But which of us children stands
his world coming forever third?
The maid presumes to the throne
sweeping before her the loose drift
    of so many poems largely abstract
    that slip in the pocket of a corpse

"Jacques Vaché used to take André Breton on crawls
of cinemas to watch fragments of film at random"
– Rose Frankhill, *A Charming History of Surrealism*

The police were in the act of being about to ask questions later. She plucked at his lapel as she kissed him to sniff his breath. The intercut police were still saving their voices. We stood this for half a reel, then panned nextdoor to find the same music-lover passing weighty violas to his business associates, whereupon a special effect of bleached Mozart caused him to fall eight storeys onto soft cars. The body may perish but the cash survives.

Cutaway to street; stopping down against the glare, and round the corner the iris relaxes back into the dark where two language-users rode the moving surface bareback, only to make their exit on a slow dissolve. What mad pursuit? I whispered. Don't take it personally said the usherette as she tore my admission in half and winked us towards the light, the screen goddess, the lily of the valley opening at speed. Strictly speaking, nothing moves in flicks.

I couldn't help thinking the last footage was the end. Neither was about to splice, neither was a woman, but they held hands in a grainy nimbus with the orange as a point of reference, the orange still somehow contriving its moments of the truly expected. The only real danger, Jacques replied, is the scene of The Artist at Work, the manic doctor in the cutting-room who cannot bear to part with a long rush telling children for instance that bees are a kind of housewife.

We have stripped beginnings of privilege, but that first sequence of the afternoon – the one with the child with big eyes and nasty secrets – surely set some kind of tone, making it harder for posterity to resist the orangepeel blinking from the gutter as we debouched into day. The kerb's our conductor rail, Jacques proclaimed as I followed him to the next fleapit. All that velvet. Those classical draperies. Those tasselled loops. We fled before they had a chance to part.

3   LOVE POEMS MUST BE MUTUAL

Paul Eluard burns with actinic light
Holding the negative up
To the window in stubby fingers
And the trees concealed in the suitcase lining
Are solid with light as they are in life
Continual poetry spilling over
Its beginnings
Eluding roadblocks
Pouring
From title to title in phosphorescent weirs
As he suckles at the left
Margin drawing line after line
From nothing
To see
The world with new eyes the eyes of the couple
To state the world with all the energies
Of childhood disappointment
To see the world
By the corona of its total eclipse

TO ERATO
Muse of Erotic Poetry

Throughout the family illness doors
are slamming like ears

The mirror weeps
and from the picture rails flock
    the miracle coordinates
        of private language

Tactful engine I would be your
thoughtful fanatic

Since I cannot find a dozen readers
let me have one
and let us speak the open leaved
    riddle of generation

THE SKIN SPEAKS

As I print out your body lying under mine
you could read my lines who, being as deep as your beauty
am pulled into so many faces for your friends

I feel for you in snow and fire
and how I suffer your every brush and blade!
I handle your goods and chattels,
I am duly touched by your family

You and I are all but inseparable
though a good hiding could scare me away. Forfend
that you that thinks I'm you
should see yourself raw as you are

No thinking but I contain it. No thinking
when I turn to wax. Without me, his body's bandage,
Mankind is but a walking wound

READ ME

for Peter Jay for his 'Life of the Pawn'

Who names me breaks me
(Silence). You can break me

but not touch me (Promise).
You can't touch me but

you can hold me (Conversation).
However I
                may be hot
                but that isn't the reason

                I may be heavy
                but that isn't the reason
you can't hold me for long –

(Breath).

You've been to school
so tell me who I am!

I invented paper
I am also a remarkable architect

yet you throw me out of the window
just because I'm fond of marmalade

and (the sting in the tail)
you even forget my name

The Wasp.

The white washed
doorless wall
    surrounding an orange
is one thing
    and easy to crack

Egg (traditional),

but I
am another

Like a latch
I am the same as understanding

so that when a squirrel runs
to the very tip of a branch of one tree and

leaps
    to another

it is for me
    to give and receive

Twig.

Steely and piercing I
am pierced through

Can't you guess?

You will need
  patience with me
as I am diving
  under and out
      a flippant porpoise
       – you may wonder –
      drawing blood
       then giving it back
You may think me
  common enough
My work is on
  the seamy side
      I draw together
      Without me
      each nicebice
       would fall into bits
You will need
  to mind your nails
for I can be
  a thorn in the flesh
      Since I was
       the bone of a fish
      I have shuttled
      and I have slaved
You with the hand
  will need a sharp eye
to keep to the point
  such as my one
      Common enough
      but look sharp!
      What is this creature's
      common name?
You've lost the thread
  I don't blame you
for truly I am
  unconscionable

The pierced piercer.

You could catch a snake
in the fork of my legs
sooner than tell my name
although you have seen me
hundreds of times

I am of gypsy stock
I come from the forest
I dance on the tightrope
My clothes are humble
and my clothes are fine

My assistant hands me up
each costume from a basket
cracks a scarf like a whip
and there appears a rainbow
in a veil of droplets

I dance on the rope above
until the sun goes in
or the wind falls or the rain
So much depends upon
me whom nobody knows

A clothespeg, of course.

In my fragility I bear your loads
I am fixed so I change in a flash

I have been so faithful
I serve any who comes along

and in my simplicity
I can paint perfect works of art

but for all that I have seen
I touch
nothing but rags

You that are so strong
so versatile and wise
and possess what you look upon

rid me of longing
read my riddle right
and I will double your wealth

Mirror.

A sack holds me
though ships can't unload me

I dog your heels

You can't walk without me
yet you have no need of me

and whether you guess me or not
you will join me at last

lying out of the sun

Shadow.

And I
am something that has been changed

Once I was green and springy
Then I was brown and tough
Next I was red and brittle
At last I am soft and grey

I am so light
one snowflake does not rest
so gently upon another

so gentle that one
downy feather is not so light
against another
on a pigeon's breast

I have been changed indeed
and now I am finished

Once green and lively
I have been made use of
and now they treat me like dirt

a light grey slight soft and falling thing
yet if you weighed me in the balance
you would find me of more weight
than that from which I was made

Who am I then?
Tell me quick
before I am brushed away

MISTRUST OF LIMESTONE : A GROTESQUE

There was a deep unearthly boom, home shuddered,
Tree went into shock, and what we half-know could happen
　　But not here, not thinkably to us, occurred
To Lucio and his twentyseven goats swallowed up

　　With the collapsing land. Immense and sickening,
The chasm gaped in an olivegrove where no mines ran,
　　A jagged mouth of darkness that without sound
Continued to consume the thrown or odd falling stone.

　　Water was guilty, and underlying beds
Full of faults, they taught the village with its awkward sense
　　Of sin that for decades tried to fill that hideous pit
With all the rubbish it deserved, until this madman

　　With a torch in his forehead tackled the black,
Pried the sidecaves, mapped the fossil river's treachery
　　Roofed with farms, and traced its every furtive stream
So olive gnarls, revets of prickly pears, a few figs

　　And that vast sinkhole could now be sold off cheap,
The groves grubbed, the spot refenced, the great gap rimmed
　　　　　　　　　　　　　　　　　　　　with brick,
　　Generations of peasant refuse hoisted,
Bats shooed out, making for stairs on an infernal scale

　　To publish this debris of drip and ooze
– *It is cold underground. A pullover is advised*,
　　The turnstiles clack; *No graffiti please. Respect
The work of millennia*, the souvenir booths respond –

　　To let the adults dabble in abandoned
Levels of desire, browse the instinctual archive, reading
　　Madonnas, towers, but mostly vegetables,
In the limbless draperies of unwondering stone.

Are clammy kilometres of kettle-fur
Truly various? – The cold millennia exude
	Slimy veils of their random Limestone stuff.
Crowds trudge the vague metro, sucking icecream stalagmites.

	Yet the tourists know what has been built of this
And what its kilned cognate can cement; what furnace it,
	Being deadburned, lined can fuse; what wings may run
On ways that it hardcores. And what the confused sibling

	Decorously recollects in letters cut
On white surfaces that shameless sweatless feet have crossed
	More silently than wood, deeds later limelit;
And of the poisons following in cylinders on trains.

	Cavers and climbers, visitor of mother
At weekend, addict of unsuffering aerial view,
	When will our zodiac mottoes urge: Live up
Nor down to nothing, but praise the Ego's witting plane,

	The dense turf around the world intensified
By almost all the talking that has ever gone on,
	Crafty knowhow of canvas and dovetail joint,
Level crossing, fanvault cavern, Lucio and his goats,

	Glass houses and scant relation to plans,
All canals, most striving for effect, just about all
	Conduct of meetings, blood donors, floppy disks,
Innocence until proved guilty, the Great Vowel Shift –

	By the fertile layer of party tricks and forms
Of government, artificial beauty of the fields,
	Moveable type, the overt stream's reluctant
Tribute to the undercourses nibbling at our crust?

SCENE IN TUSCANY

It is spring and in the thin leaf
the grain of every thing is more distinct.
    The parts of corn, hardly in shoot,
leave their furrows clear. Fringing rushes let
    streams flow right up to their edges.

A dove flops into the pock of a wall
    of a fortified clump of farm,
tower, and one-room church with curly tiles.
    Winter's hay carved to the spindle,
a whole lemontree stunted in a tub,

    watch the valley and opposing
slopes, violet folded hills calm as lips
    in the slight mist that varies tints
misty but never mixed as they come down
    to olive thickets and blond clays,

taking up scattered pieces of young crops,
    gingery willows in half-bud
fuzzing to a bit of a pink orchard
    and a bit of white freshly pruned,
fluttering rags to civilise the birds.

    It is morning; the labourers
can be picked out among trim lines of stakes
    moulded to the valley contours,
tying the as yet leafless vines that comb
    to sky-edging dabbed with small trees.

The details are being trained, buds chosen.
    To every tendril its clipping.
A black-shawled woman bundles the snippets.
    Olive brishings heap by the path
as symbol of the season and its task.

The thigh-stump of a polled willow
holds taut the twine for shoots of this vintage
     to creep along, its own shoots cropped
for the twists of springy twig, skilled device
     clipping the young to the old vine.

A shiny cock is standing on a wheel.
     Scrap, shred, wisp, wedge, strip of colour
is intrinsic as leafing bud. It is
     almost time for Western landscape
painting to begin, its long displacement.

TIMES THAT SPOKE OF THE FUTURE

from two poems by Franco Fortini

1   ARMISTICE, 1943

Coppery moon. Coarse from the field, hair scorched,
women sweeten in limewashed villages.

Sand at street-taps cleaning clinking mess tins.
On the Milan road two workers, three girls

dance on gleaming tar – spittle of phosphor –
one shout of frightened joy. All the women

talking with conscripts disbanded in files
of vines. Over cities, sour wine of song.

Weak fire of the radio. Anything
could happen. Those due to die tomorrow

drink from trickling iron pumps at the stations.
Sleep on straw, clutching guns. Summer shrivels

from Turin to Salerno. It's all gone;
we're free to escape, to ignore, to weep.

2   THE ENGLISH CEMETERY

Also now
     – evening, October
     and through the avenues the mist
        (but lightly)
     veiling the plane trees
        as in those times of ours
     walled in ivy and cypress –
the keepers
are burning twigs and dry laurels.
                Green
the smoke, like that from charcoal burners
in the mountains.

        They would die
those evenings, already chill
        and I
would search for your wrist to stroke.
              Then
were the uncertain lights, large shadows
of gardens, your firm step on the gravel,
and the stone of the iron gates
    (you used to say)
had the smell of October in it
    the smoke
tasted of the wine harvest
and your mouth
        opened itself in the dark
           a slow grape.

Now, perhaps, I would not recognise
your form.
I suppose you are alive
                              and think sometimes
of how much passed between us
and of how much is passed

                    and from time to time
a longing such as may sigh in the poor dead
     to go back
                         to see the one you were

walking again in those evenings of a time
which has no place
                         even though
I am walking down these avenues of Florence where
                                        the mist
                    (but lightly)
     veils the plane trees
and in the gardens burn
the laurel fires.

"AND ALL WENT TO BE TAXED"

for Barbara Garvin

A city of stony fields, reticent people,
the thornbush stunted, slanted by seawind,
any driftwood going to gate or roofing slat,
the smaller gathered for kindlingwood;

strangers noticed a mile down the road;
the children hiding from a strange lorry,
on watch as the periwinkles gathered
by them in sacks are weighed on a yard;

men talking in huddles by a stone fence
blocked with flotsam seeming to strangers
close as shellfish, closed as axioms,
lidding their pipes with bottle-lids:

string from a parcel will go to hold
a gàte together, the new sacks the grain
comes in will dampcourse a rick of straw;
and turf ricked neatly as a slane turns.

A yard of fowl have their grain scattered
by children clucking and calling pet names
to a granite slab that crops up in grass
as the lined palm that bases the cottage

as the mother keeps knots on every thread
and just now sets a geranium pot
in the red-silled window in the thick white
walls that keep the secret of all these

who propagate as secretly as ferns.

The candle grains the limewashed stone like wood,
being the strongest light. Drawing its watchers
as in dawn or evening light, the shadow reveals,
bringing to fabric what our affection brings,
converting sight into a touching sense,
as it is the raking light discloses
the painter's gesture and repented form.

Candleflame in virtue of its weakness
will search like fingertips the patina
as written as a hand, worked and worked over,
the skindeep scratches and workings-even
cracked and filled, smutched and smoothed-against
in the crust of lime with insects bedded in
and the fossil of a paintbrush whisker

enhanced now by the obliquely feeling light
as it casts the grain, resolving the room
to a reddish-yellow order that has the art
of graining stone like a working tabletop,
turning the shadows to a rippling sense,
a handscape falling out with authority
by its love of all that is variable;

and such the walls return, each granule
within the glowing body of the recess,
as though their width were made of nothing else
but mild candlelight, composed of flickering,
edging onto the window's geranium lip and at this
familiar horizon cutting to black, to pulse
across that wide unsearchable where it is not.

Luke 2:1-3
JOSEPHUS
Antiq. XVIII,
1,1
And there went out a decree
that all the world should be taxed
and at first the Jews cut up rough
but the blind overseer calmed them, MILTON
Lyc. 119
Joasar the highpriest, explaining
"the necessity of the arrangements"
that they be taxed on salt and meat,
work the land for the foreigner
Luke 20:25 and render on the roads to Caesar.

Acts 5:37;
JOS. loc. cit.
& Bellum
II.viii,1
Yet there was one Judas
of Galilee, who saw a census
preparing for Roman taxes prepared
for enslavement, and nations have
to assert their freedom in arms. PEARSE Proc.
1916; JOS.
Antiq. loc. cit.
JOS. loc. cit. No man should submit to mortal man
as Lord, nor should the word
GRAETZ
II.134 of any taxgatherer be honoured
nor his testimony any more.

Rev. Patrick S. Dinneen, *Foclóir Gaedilge agus Béarla, An Irish-English Dictionary* (The Irish Texts Society, Dublin 1975 [1904]).

H. Graetz, *History of the Jews* II (The Jewish Publication Society of America, Philadelphia 1893).

Flavius Josephus, *Antiquitates Judaicae* (Antiquities of the Jews) and *Bellum Judaicum* (The History of the Destruction of Jerusalem), translated by William Whiston (London, 1895).

Seán Mac Giollarnáth, *Conamara* (Cork, n.d.).

Patrick Pearse, *Proclamation of the Irish Republic* (Dublin, Easter 1916).

And this Judas asked the Jews:
What are you talking in whispers for?

JOS. *Bellum*
II.viii,1

and whether, if there could be any
amongst them put up with declaring
for such a tax, they would declare
anything but cowardice.

Acts loc. cit.

And this Judas was able with such talk
to gather many people after him

I.e. candle
or flash of
anger: *vide*
DINNEEN
226

and light a *coinneal* amongst them.

So it came to pass that for this
"inviolable love of freedom"
this Judas was snuffed out

JOS. *Antiq.*
XVIII,i,6
Acts loc. cit.

JOS. *Antiq.*
XX,v,2

and all his sons; and their rebellion
gave to Jerusalem for the first time
an entire Roman legion stationed
to retain the City of Jerusalem,
and the number of the crucified

GRAETZ
II.126

amounted to some 2,000.

JOS. *Antiq.*
XVIII,i,1

And after that, says Joseph
ben Mathias called Flavius Josephus,
one brutal war came down upon us
after another, and we lost our friends
who had used to soften our adversity
and there was pillage and murder
of our principal men, whence arose
further seditions, and murders
which fell sometimes on the enemy.

JOS. *Antiq.*
XVIII,i,1

And then the Famine came amongst us
that brought us to despair;

so it is not to the doorstep preacher that people expect
for the springs of former content to be running again
the wilderness and the lonely place to blossom with shops
for the Galway road to be straightened out
the stones of Conamara ironed out
as creases from a shirt

for the sailing boats to be fishing the islands again
for the Bens to be made low and the bogs of Ireland drained
and tended with gardens with fruit between the rows of fruit
and the furthest islands bridged to the main
the deserted islands roofed and returned
the long divided joined

nor for the voice of the Gaelic to be heard through the land
nor yet for the prayers of the living to be empowered
to rouse the dead
                and bring the scattered home
as we dream the ones who are lost and gone
are home and swimming in the rivermouth
and in the breaking wave

as candle light

is touching down across the stony fields
and even out to sea, received as harbour light,   DINNEEN
and any reddish star is clinging to the coast   226
as lights in network are strung around the bay,
making tracks between clusters and outliers,
reflecting the fishing-boats lit like a village,

so many candles interlacing haggards and lanes.
The mild flame in the four-paned gable window sees
to what height the rock can be pressed into bearing,
traces the contours of shepherds, mountainy men
keeping their sheep inland, and the crescent of bedrock
of glowing islands in line with the coastal hills

– a tally of candles and all that goes searching in them,
as the outlandish appear from slope and bogland
hidden by day, and watchful children at windows
point them out by name, to the farthest window,
even the newcomers, even the guards, picked out
by candles, by children, by name, like so many stars

on January the 5th, Eve of the Epiphany,
when the real cold weather begins
and hay to be forked out into the fields

when the head of the house would pound
the bread of adversity
against the windows and barred doors
that Famine might pass them by that year

Isaiah 30:20;
*Journ.Roy.Soc.
Ant.Ire.* 1853,
146

and when the next harvest is the sea rods
and some admiring candles watch the sea,
sensing night that offers its coastal tang
in fifty modes as subtle as snow or sand,
to turn the shadows into a rippling sense

on January the 5th, Eve of Epiphany,
Twelfth Night of Christmas, *Nollaig na mBan*,
Anniversary of the Big Wind, the windows each
to each recover flickering connecting lights
along the heights from Coillín to Calafínis head
and to Fínis island and Muigh Inis

i.e. "Women's
Christmas" –
DINNEEN 799

and from Coillín to Leitirdeiscirt,
Roisín a'Tomha, Carna, Síduach,
and Ruisínnamainiach and all the world
of Iorrus Aithneach constellating itself
to itself as it goes with all the world to be taxed.

MAC GIOLL-
ARNÁTH
54,56

ADVICE TO A RULER

Sir, the present life of man
in the face of unknown time
seems like this:
                    a winter's night,
you at supper with your wise
and strong men, a hearty fire
warming the room, while outside
rage storms of hail and rain

and this lonely sparrow comes fluttering in,
flits out again...
                    In through this door
and out by that.
                    For the time being
shielded from Winter's anger,
his refuge passes in a flash

winging from winter into winter
we lose him from our glimpse of light
into that darkness, as he came.

FROM THE PRISON QUATRAINS
OF HO CHI MINH

In 1941, Nguyen Sinh Cung entered China to contact Chiang Kai-shek on behalf of the newly founded Viet Minh. For the purpose he pretended to be blind and he had printed on some visiting cards his latest pseudonym – Ho Chi Minh, meaning The One Who Enlightens.

But meanwhile, the 'warlord' Chang Fa-kwei had shifted his patronage to the pro-Kuomintang Vietnamese group; and so 'Ho Chi Minh' came to be imprisoned in various gaols, with forced marches between. Amongst the fruits are some hundred and twenty poems that have come to be called the *Prison Diary* of Ho Chi Minh.

I take these details from the biography by Charles Fenn, who writes that the poems "are not really a diary, but impressions; some descriptive, others more abstract. He wrote them, not in Vietnamese, but in classical Chinese. Perhaps he felt it was better that his guards should be able to read what he was writing; perhaps he merely felt the need to exercise the discipline...".[1] Moreover, some of them embodied messages to his comrades as to his whereabouts and state of mind.[2]

Of their literary quality I think we may be assured. Ho Chi Minh's polemical prose is part of the history of modern writing in Vietnamese: "his language has the simplicity, the apparent naïveté, of folk thinking. He advanced his teachings in the manner of the village storytellers."[3] His style is "lively, crisp, concise, often humour-tinged".[4] It is a cultural act of genius that these concrete qualities should also be fed by the poetics of Mandarin Chinese. "The humanistic tradition of the classic literature, with its striving for justice, for conditions worthy of human beings, was carried over into a consciously political task."[5]

Hanoi published a translation of the prison poems into regular English quatrains by Aileen Palmer (*Prison Diary*, 1965). As I selected and re-arranged these translations for a public reading, I found I needed to tamper with the diction and rhythm, and eventually to rework then in a denser and more imagistic verse-form. Then for about five years I lost her valuable book, but continued to tinker with the poems as though they were my own, so they have grown away from their originals. Nevertheless, I have tried to be true to the qualities that drew me to them in the first place. Strictly speaking, the result is a dialogue between the official translation and a conflicting poetic style; but the subject is Ho Chi Minh.

1   *Ho Chi Minh* (London, 1973), p.71.
2   See William Warbey, *Vietnam: The Truth* (London, 1965), pp.41-2.
3   Peter Weiss, *Notes on the Cultural Life of the Democratic Republic of Vietnam* (London, 1971), p.48.
4   Note in Ho Chi Minh, *Selected Writings 1920-1969* (Hanoi, 1973), p.7.
5   Weiss, p.48.

PRISON QUATRAINS

Borne by the stream
   the boat glides on
My legs roped ·
   to a roofbeam gibbet

Along the banks
   are thriving villages
as the fishing boat glides
   midstream

———

Force-marched
thirty miles today
shirt soaking
shoes splitting

All night long
nowhere to lie
I wait for another day like this
   hunched by a dungheap

———

Although my limbs
   are tied well enough
I can hear the birds
   and smell the woods in spring

Who can stop me
   enjoying these
that take from a long trek some
   of its loneliness?

Branches fretted
   by freezing blades
   Remote gongs
      drawing us on

Flutes played
   by droving boys
as they drive their buffaloes along
      the dusk

———

Ropes give way
   to ringing irons
as though I were decked
    with showy rings of jade

The convict steps
   with all the dignity
of an ancient court official
    and all his restraint

———

Always the same
bowl of rice
no greens no tea

Every man in this establishment is free

to wash his face
   and give up tea
or want the tea
   and neglect his face

The wife of a conscript deserter
   has to say:

You left me
   in our room
with grief for my only friend

   So the authorities
took pity and assisted me
   to one of their several gaols

———

Gamblers
   promptly arrested
once inside
   bet as they please

Can this be why
   one always hears it asked
Why the hell didn't I think
   of coming here before?

———

Sleepless autumn night
no mattress
no blanket
the curled body

Moonlight on the bank
only deepens the cold
the Pole Star peering in at us
through bars

The sudden note
   of one more in gaol
the nostalgic note of the flute
   weepingly swells

across rivers and mountains
   and we seem to watch
her climbing that distant rock
   to watch for our return

―――――

And one who was just
   ounces of skin and bone

His end was cold
   hunger and sadness of heart

Only last night
   he slept by my side

This morning he has taken himself
   on a frightening journey to the land of nine springs

―――――

While birds are seeking
   the woods to rest
a girl in a far village
   is grinding maize

When all this maize
   is ground
     the oven will
       burn red

Ten years age you less
than a season in here
never eating your fill
never washing all over

So
   I have lost a tooth
and colour of hair
I have gained scabies
   and a certain resolve

———

Poets used to sing
   of snows and flowers
of moonlight and the wind
   across the moon

Reaching today
   we construct
poems in steel
   and craft leads attacks

———

How each grain
   of rice must suffer
under the pestle's pounding
   to become so white

With man in this world
   the lathe of misfortune
is turning us into
   polished jade

Another hungry mouth
bites each night
at the right ankle
leaving the left sleepily to stretch

Stranger still
to clamour to be clapped in irons
and then be able
to sleep in peace

———

A constellation trails
from the summit
or the song of the cricket dies or returns
to tell the year

What could the prisoner care
what season it is?
Only for the spring of freedom
   His and his people's

———

On release I walk in the mountains
   the clouds hugging the peaks
the peaks embracing the clouds
      the river gleaming as a cleaned blade

Along the crest of the mountains
   my mind clears
as I wander looking to the western sky
      and think of all my old friends

ACKNOWLEDGEMENTS

Barbara Garvin helped me with Franco Fortini's Italian, and the poet has kindly encouraged our efforts. Maria Dotsika Papavasiliou gave me literal versions from the Greek of Ritsos. But the results, in both cases, are too free to be called translations. I gratefully acknowledge my debt to Aileen Palmer and the Foreign Languages Publishing House, Hanoi, on whose text I have based my selected versions from Ho Chi Minh's *Prison Diary*. The 'Advice' to Edwin, King of Northumbria, is based on a speech from The Venerable Bede's *Historia Ecclesiastica* II, xiii.

I am also grateful to the following editors and critical friends: Isobel Armstrong, Jacques Berthoud, Les Harrop, Peter Jay, Jenny Lindford, David Moody, David Rankin, Julia Sterland, Simeon Underwood and Judith Woolf. Hugh Haughton's acute comments have been particularly genial.

The title of the collection I owe to a *T.L.S.* reviewer (16/5/80) who, noticing that one of my pieces had been commissioned by a Romanian newspaper, reported that this "confirms one's worst suspicions".